PRAISE FOR LEAD YOUR TIME

"I know Cletous as a man of value and principles, who knows how to manage his time wisely. As he quoted that time is the greatest asset we have in life, if we don't know what to do with it someone else may use it wrongly.

I encourage everyone to read this book and I believe it will change lives of many."

Pastor John A Manpuele

LEAD YOUR TIME

Time is

your best

resource

To My Friend
DEREK

CLETOUS KASOMBO

LEAD YOUR TIME
Copyright © 2014 by Cletous Kasombo

ISBN: 978-1-4866-0464-7

Word Alive Press
131 Cordite Road, Winnipeg, MB R3W 1S1
www.wordalivepress.ca

WORD ALIVE
—P R E S S—

Cataloguing in Publication may be obtained through Library and Archives Canada

DEDICATION

To my brother, Pascal (Cera) who is a true leader wherever he goes. I thank you. I have realized that you are not only a brother to me but my best friend, also. The funny thing is that sometimes I consider you to be my mentor, and some other times you are my protégé. I love you, brother.

Contents

ACKNOWLEDGEMENTS

In writing this book, it's my great pleasure to thank my siblings, who are close to me, not only because we have the same parents but also because we grew up sharing beds, dishes, and many other things that bond us together—Jean Pierre, Sophie, Jean Claude, Martin, Willy, Pascal (Cera), Patrick, Eric, Tony, and Muss. These are my next of kin. All of us come from the same womb, of my mother, Adele. I love you, Mom.

In our family of eleven, where ten are boys, it was easy to fight for peanuts, just as it was for money. In spite of all our childhood fights, my mom tried to remind us that we are and must remain a loving family. Yes, Mom, it hasn't been easy for you, but you have made it.

I remind my brothers of this word: *karindula*. It doesn't make sense to anyone unless you know the meaning of *chituru*. We've survived very tough situations. I love you so much, brothers.

To all the Manzo, who have been more like family than friends, I say thank you. Thank you to all my friends who made it possible for me to write this book—I mean Pappy-Mukalay, Yve-Tshamala, among others. I also say thank you to those who have changed my life by what they've said and written, and how they've lived their lives.

Among my many influences are Anthony Robbins; Barry, Joyce, and Jason Boucher; Creflo Dollar; P. Felix; Frank; Jerry Savelle; Jesse Duplantis; Joyce Meyer; John Maxwell; John Mason; John Hagee; Gene Norman; Myles Munroe; Peter Daniels; Rob Thompson; Ray McCauley; Robert H. Schuller; Tim Storey, Zig Ziglar, P. Theo; Bev Wolmarans; P. Veyi-Nkossi; Peter Youngren; T.D. Jakes; Rod Parsley; Eddie Long; James and Betty Robinson; Paula White; David Molapo; Joel Osteen; and Joseph Prince.

If I were to thank everyone, half of this book would be filled with names. For those who choose to read this book now, however, I mean to thank you—not because you've bought my book, but because you've decided to read it. I will say this with my tongue in cheek: what would be the reason of having a bridge between two cities if nobody decided to cross the border?

I finally thank God for giving me Kasongo-Michel as my father. He has been a motivational leader for all of his children. More than our father, he has been our friend, always teaching us to be relentless, even in the toughest situations, because "sooner or later, we are going to make it." This was among his most preferred pieces of advice. Indeed, his words of direction have made us who we are today.

To Jean Claude, who has been my mentor for a long time, I say thank you. I am able to write today because he taught me to read. That's a fact. I could never have been able to write a book without reading one first.

INTRODUCTION

When I was younger, my father was dismissed from work because of his manager's mistake. Without work, there is neither wages nor income. Fortunately, my brothers and I knew how to deal with the bush; we became hunters to feed our parents. Thank God it was a brief moment. Our mother took the weight upon her shoulders when she found a field. After cultivating it and sowing seeds, we couldn't believe what she was doing. One day, we were amazed to see the harvest—maize, beans, peanut, sweet potato, you name it. She fed us all, including our father. Feeding the family became a cycle, from the father to the mother, and then to the children.

Think about this. Early in the morning, the bell rings in your bedroom, the sound going straight to your ears. Your brain receives the message and tells your eyes to open, and your legs to stand. Another message tells your legs to walk into the bathroom, where your hands turn on the hot water in the bath. But when your feet enter the bath, you feel the water too hot. So you add cold water. Your eyes see the white soap as you wash your body; unfortunately, the smell gets into your nostrils, which tell you that it's not the usual soap. After a pleasant bath, you leave the bathroom with a smile on your face.

Remember that each part of your body was involved in the process. Life can be considered in this way. It doesn't make sense to talk about time without knowing that there's no life outside of time. I invite you for a journey in which we will discover the reason we've been created.

LEAD YOUR TIME

Time is a gift. So is life. Whether you play with or respect life depends on you, but you better know that there'll be a reward if you respect it. So why play with it? Your time has the potential to produce whatever desire you have. You can become whatever you want to be. The choice is yours, because your life belongs to you.

Whatever you do with it, the outcome will either impress or depress you. However, time is important—so important that you don't want to lose even one second. What you are right now is the result of the way you handled yesterday's time. In theory, I can earn an infinite amount of money, but the time in which to do it is limited. I must therefore be careful with my time.

If you ask me for twenty dollars, I'll give it to you. If you ask for twenty minutes of my time, I'll think twice. I value time more than anything. I would try to squeeze twenty-six hours into the day, were it possible. It's easy to make twenty dollars, but it's impossible to get back a lost minute. If you lose it, it's gone. You can't get it back.

This is why I advise you not to play with time. Time is not money, as we've been taught, though you need time to do all things. With this understanding, you may agree that the result of time isn't instantaneous. It's a process.

You can go to a casino and win a million-dollar jackpot, but if I ask you to recreate that success, you may tell me that you can't; after all, it was just a lucky break. But progress comes with process. For instance, when a construction company plans to build five hundred homes, fifty per year, the amount of money received in the first year will definitely be the same as the last year of the contract. Time isn't the same as money; we don't have to put money and time on the same level as if they have equivalence.

When we say time is money, it means that life depends on time. We can have billions of dollars, but we can never buy a minute. What's the pleasure of having money without living? With money, you have the option to live in a beautiful house, wherever you want it, and however you want it. But when it comes to time, you don't have control. You don't know what the future holds. After all, you must work in order to expect money. Money comes after work, and you must spend time in order to work. Money becomes a consequence of how you use your time. Time pays off.

You Have a Short Moment

O pportunity isn't always available. That's why we call it opportunity. However, we have the ability to reject or neglect any opportunity that comes our way, because we have the choice whether to accept or refuse it.

The most precious resource you have is your time. If even one minute is lost, you might think to get it back. Unfortunately, you can't. You can rush around, putting yourself at great risk and peril trying to get something you'll never get back. Regret not the moment you lost your time. Instead consider the time you've got left and make it more valuable. We all have twenty-four hours a day, seven days a week, thirty or so days a month, and twelve months a year.

Some of us live a hundred years, others twenty, while still others may only live five. The fulfillment of our purpose is not measured by age. When I was a young boy, every time my teacher taught a lesson, as students we wouldn't all understand it the same way. The proof is that if you go into any class at the end of a school year, the students are given grades. One student is so-called first, another so-called second, and at the bottom some-one is so-called last.[1] In school, the teacher always takes the same length of time, utilizes the same strategy to explain the same lesson to all the students.

But what made each pupil or student catch the lesson in his own way?

---

1 Excuse me if I call them "so-called." After long study and research, I have realized that there is neither first nor last in life. We are all the firsts in our uniqueness, though different in talents.

UNITY IN DIVERSITY

I f you surround yourself with people who are like you, you'll have no clue what you're missing and the danger you're putting yourself in. People who are just like you will compete with you, but those who are different will *complete* you.

I thank God because He made us unique. God never created two persons alike. Nobody on this earth has your fingerprint. Nobody acts exactly like you. This means that you're unique on the face of the earth, among a global population of approximately 7.2 billion people. You are different from all others, but the reason you're unique is to be united with others. What would be the reason for being united if we were the same in all aspects of life?

The reason for diversity is to create unity. On the eve of New Year 2000, I was amazed to see different people, in different countries, in different ways, using different fireworks to celebrate the same event. Even though the fireworks weren't the same everywhere, at least it was for the same event and purpose.

In the world today, if you have to invent a product, you must make sure it corresponds to a certain standard, otherwise your product will miss the market. This is proof that there's a sense of unity within us, a unity which we often fail to release. Our perception of others is often tainted with distrust and suspicion.

Hydrogen will never make water by itself; neither will oxygen by itself make water. But if hydrogen (H2) is combined with oxygen (O), we will produce water (H2O). Consider what the output of man with man would be, or the output of woman with woman. No, you must have a man with woman. Even when God created man, He realized that a man needs somebody else to complete him. So He said, *"I will make him a helper (suitable, adapted, complementary) for him"* (Genesis 2:18).

One day, I went to watch a hockey match in Ottawa. The Senators were playing the New York Islanders. While the two teams played, an idea came to mind: all the players were running after a small piece of rubber (a puck). A minute later, the two teams started fighting—a real, physical fight—and I could tell that this wasn't hockey but a battlefield. I could see blood all over the ice. I said to myself, *What is this? Why doesn't each player have their own puck?* I understood later that it was the rule of the game. The winner was the one who struck the most goals into the opponent's net.

Fortunately, real life isn't like this. In essence, we don't run after a puck; we all have our own puck right in front of us. The decision to shoot it is ours. Everybody has their individual puck which must be struck into the net. In life, there is no coach, no judge. Imagine being your own referee. Indeed, you're both the judge and spectator.

Be prepared to stand by your conviction. Be yourself and aim for excellence, because the best you can be is within you. There is no doubt that you'll win. You will, for sure.

The puck is on your stick. The net is wide open in front of you. The funny thing is that there's no one to prevent you from playing the game which you are bound to win. Play now—and win.

GIVE WHAT YOU HAVE

Y ou don't have to ask what you can give to the world. Understand that you have a precious gift to give, and the world will never expect from you something you don't have. No one can see as you see; no one is able to do things exactly your way.

This world doesn't need what you don't have. Give what you have and you'll be amazed at the impact it will have on others. Never neglect what you have. Can five loaves of bread and two fish feed five thousand people? Absolutely not. Whenever you give away what's in your hand, God will multiply it, making it grand and great.

What have you got? Identify what your gift is, because you can only use what you know you have. It doesn't matter what it is. Identify it, make sure it's your gift, and then give it away.

When we buy gas to put in our cars, we do it in order to burn the gas. In order for me to move my car from one point to another, the gas in the tank of my car must burn. The gas fulfills no purpose until it's gone. If you keep the gas in your tank unused for a long period of time, you'll lose it little by little. In keeping it, you might waste it.

In Matthew 25:15, a servant who received one talent from his master was afraid to use it. He finally lost it. The other two servants received even more after, because they *used* their talents.

Look around yourself. Look within yourself. There must be something special you're holding. It may be money, or it may be help. It can be an idea, but perhaps you're too afraid to let it out. It may be something you can't even speak with your mouth but have the ability to scribble down. Maybe you don't know how or where to start. It can be the ability to see things in advance. It can be a beautiful voice; perhaps you have the ability to become a great singer such as this world has never heard. It can be a constant smile; some people may think you're funny, but they don't know your potential for comedy. It can be spending quality time with others, encouraging those who need you.

The biggest asset you have is your precious time. Don't lose it.

USE YOUR GIFT

Decide to dig out what is inside of you. If you don't, someone else will wrongfully use it. Others can cry with you, but they'll never cry for you. Make a decision today to use your time profitably. Imagine that you owe somebody a large amount of money. After a while, the person cancels your debt and you're told not to pay it back. What would your reaction be after sending a gift to someone and after a while finding it not only unused but also abused? Before answering, you better know what you're doing with your time.

Can you at least recognize what you have? If you don't know what you have, you'll never be able to benefit from it. And if you judge not to use it, somebody else might wrongfully use it.

On August 6, 1945, the United States launched two atomic bombs on Japan, in Nagasaki and Hiroshima. The uranium used to make those bombs was extracted in Shinkolobwe, a small village approximately thirty-five kilometres from my neighbourhood in the province of Katanga, in the Democratic Republic of Congo. Since that time, I've had a bad feeling knowing that people perished because of what we possess in our country. Someone used it for destruction and annihilation. Although we possess a good quality and quantity of uranium, we were controlled by the United States. Even though it was ours, we could do very little. What a pity! The United States could even decide to use it against us, and no one would stop them.

Uranium can be used in radiology, in nuclear energy, for nuclear reactors and submarines, and in many other domains. It's absolutely fantastic to hear of these technologies, but the fact is that the same uranium can be used to make bombs. A bomb can flatten cities, destroy lives, and devastate the environment beyond repair. All these are consequences of not using what we have.

DIE EMPTY

You are unique, and there is no one like you. This is why the only person who can do what you're supposed to do is you. If you don't use your time to tap into your potential, the world will lack that which only you can give. I don't know any other way people can hear my voice if I don't speak. One must be heard through speaking. Sometimes starting something can look funny. People around you may think you're crazy. The crowd won't encourage you. They may discourage you because they don't want to lose your company, so make sure you don't look like them, even if you decide to be with them. Don't wait until they give you a microphone to speak; if the microphone is held by your adversary, he won't allow you to have it until you do something.

There are millions of ideas in people's heads which go unused. Don't go to the grave with ideas in your head. According to Dr. Myles Munroe, the greatest tragedy in life isn't death, but life without a purpose. I say it this way: it's more tragic to live and not know why than it is to die and not know life.

The richest land on earth is not Gauteng Province in South Africa, although it contains substantial gold and diamonds. Neither is it the Democratic Republic of Congo, with all its mineral products. The richest territory is neither found in Russia, Saudi Arabia, the United States, Iran, China, Mexico, Canada, or the United Arab Emirates. These are the top eight producers of oil in the world. The richest field is not where we find all these natural resources, though everybody has their eyes fixed on them.

We neglect the most important place, which contains a resource we have never seen and will never be able to see—the cemetery. Hold your breath for a second and allow me to explain.

In the cemetery lies books that have never been written, songs that have never been sung, ideas that have never been known, medications that have never been produced, houses that have never been built, and companies that have never seen the light of day. They were just ideas in the heads of people who went to the grave without sharing them.

The world faces many challenges these days, and the answer is in the grave. What a shame! The cemetery is rich. Please don't be one of those who enriches the cemetery. You need to die empty.

Rick Warren once said that it's not a sin to live wealthy, but it's a sin to die wealthy. What does it mean to die empty? It means to release the potential within you. If nobody benefits from what you possess, the grave will certainly get all of it.

You have a gift, and you need to find it. You may try to do several things in life which don't work to your expectations, but there are things you are excellent at, things you don't struggle to do. You just do them at ease, because that's your gift.

A golf club in my hand is a dangerous weapon, but the same golf club in Tiger Woods' hand produces a master champion. A hamburger in my hand is just a lunch, but the same hamburger in Ray Kroc's hand produces the fast food restaurant that feeds the world. I'm talking about McDonald's! A tennis racket in my hand is a toy that I'll hang on a wall to behold its beauty, but the same tennis racket in Venus Williams' hand produces a Wimbledon champion. A basketball in my hand is insignificant, but the same basketball in Jordan's hand produces a fifty-eight per game scorer. A steering wheel in my hands is nothing but a ride to work, but the same steering wheel in Michael Schumacher's hands produces the Formula One champion.

It all depends on whose hand it's in.

Spit and clay in my hand is just mud, but spit and clay in Jesus' hand will open the eyes of the blind. Nails in my hands are merely tools to build the roof of my house, but nails in Jesus' hands means salvation for all humanity.

I therefore realize that my life is a disaster in my own hands, but my life in God's hands can be everything I believe it to be. That will allow me to fulfill my mission on this earth. I will then boldly declare that I'm ready to die empty.

PREDICT YOUR FUTURE

A system will certainly produce results, and can also reproduce these same results over and over. According to John L. Mason, a tree that bears fruit can also guarantee its own reproduction by producing seeds which will eventually grow to become trees of their own.

But when you function with no system at all, you live by luck. How in the world can you accept living by luck? I mean, you're just sitting there hoping for good thing to happen to you!

This reminds me of one of my brothers. He was supposed to have a meeting with a manager of a certain company, but he was stopped at the gate by a security guard who happened to be very rude. This guard, for an unknown reason, wouldn't allow my brother to proceed. He wanted to make sure my brother had really been invited to the meeting.

Someone in the security office picked up his phone and called the head office, asking if anyone there had invited my brother. During this call, my brother told them,

"Don't you know that I'm capable of purchasing this company and then firing you?"

The guard laughed. "Sir, go away and make your wish."

That's totally ridiculous. When you operate with a system, it will always be possible to predict the outcome. What do I mean by this? If you plan your life, you won't be surprised by what happens, because you know where you're going. You can be aware of what you'll face along the way.

Obviously, there are things you can't predict—like sickness, accident, or death. This doesn't become an excuse to live a life of wishing things to happen. We can always plan our lives, and that requires us to work a system. Here's an interesting thing about a system: it has no friends, and it will work anywhere, anytime, and for anybody who applies it.

A breeder knows what kind of animal he or she has on his farm. He has an assurance, knowing what animal to slaughter and when he wants to do it. He can even make it happen again and again. Unfortunately, the hunter goes to the jungle unsure not only of what kind of animal he can bag, but also who is going to be the first chased—the animal or the hunter. He can catch an animal, but he doesn't ignore the fact that he can also be caught by the animal.

Even if he's lucky and survives today, there's no guarantee for tomorrow. This is because he lacks a system. Ray Kroc took time to conceive an idea and start selling hamburgers; McDonald's has a big dream to build franchises worldwide that are nearer to each other than the average distance between two gas stations. According to its statistics, one McDonald's franchise opens every ten hours somewhere in the world.

These are some examples of events and systems we need to be aware of so that we may become progressive. We always want things to work for us without putting in the time it takes to make them happen. Everything in life should come with a system. A system makes time meaningful.

Don't be a hunter, because you may also be hunted. Instead I dare you to be a breeder. Work with a system.

NOW IS THE TIME TO START

T he best time to start is now. Do what you have to do, because now is always the best time. Don't put off for later what you can do today. According to Debbie Macomber, we must pursue our dreams today. Now is the time!

Remember that today was tomorrow yesterday. You said to yourself, "I will do it tomorrow." Forget not that another tomorrow will show up tomorrow.

Dozens of the books I've read, even though they are different, say essentially the same thing: start now. One day, I was thinking about writing a book, but how would I start and what would the content be? I was clueless, at first.

Engines have the capacity to function in many conditions, but with no starter they'll never be able to perform or demonstrate how powerful they are. After making a decision to start writing this book, I found that the starting point was very important. I started with forty-five minutes each day, and later I could spend six straight hours on it, ignoring even my lunch. Writing became the most interesting thing in my world, and I would sit down and do it again and again. I didn't want to be disturbed until I finished writing all my ideas. Once an idea came to mind, it wouldn't stop until I stopped it.

We all have something to say to help others. Learn what you need to know to achieve your goal. Find out the area in which you can really show who you are. Be willing to do the best you can. You are the master of your time; you decide what to do with it. The key to your future is hidden in the time you have right now. A fruitful life isn't the result of chance but choice—right now.

Now is the best time to start, if you're willing. If you've ever thought about being a football player, now is the time. If you've ever thought about being a motor mechanic, now is the time. If you've ever thought about quitting your comfort zone, now is the time. If you've ever thought about quitting drugs, now is the time. If you've ever thought about receiving Jesus as your personal saviour, now is the time.

Remember: the present time is at your disposal, but the next few seconds belong to God. So make the right decision. Now.

Do Not Quit

I've never denied that I could go through pain in my life, but I've always believed that the trouble I go through has an end. However, there's no way to see an exit out of trouble if we're static. An exit cannot come to us; we must go and find it. In order for us to get out of tough situations, we must take action.

Many of us have heard of Walt Disney. I admire his confidence. Even in the middle of incredible pressure, he didn't quit. When Walt Disney had the idea to build Disneyland, he asked for finance. A lot of banks refused for the simple reason that they didn't think he was creative enough. He refused to change his mind, even though he couldn't find help. Knowing the potential within himself and his goal, Disney didn't care about who tried to stop him from fulfilling his destiny.

The only person's experience this world is waiting for is yours; you are a solution to one problem in this world. You have been given time, a life for a purpose, and everything that exists has a reason. The hair in your nose has purpose—to stop bacteria from reaching your lungs. This is proof that a human being must have a purpose.

The difference between you and all those who seem to be ahead of you isn't position, power, or even money. It's time.

Let's go back ten, fifteen, twenty-five years and remind ourselves what we were doing in the past. We'll probably find that we were laughing at others. Maybe we were certain about their failure and we just wanted to see the end so we could laugh out loud at them. Fortunately, we rejoice with them now. I used to wonder how I could be happy about somebody else's failure. It's easy to learn from others' success. Every time I see somebody's success, it gives me a great deal of energy, and a proven example for my own success.

While I know that others' success is going to benefit me, even if I don't reap a portion of it, why and how should I be happy of their failures? People often give up on their goals not because they cannot succeed, but because we discourage them. Few of them understand that there's a price for success.

You can fail a hundred times, but one success can make you forget all your past failures. Read the biographies of Ray Kroc, Walt Disney, Colonel Sanders, Martin Luther King, and Nelson Mandela. These people had one thing in common: they saw their failures as a platform, not a roof.

There is always a price to pay if we really need a change. All that we expect tomorrow depends on how we use what we have now. You're able to go anywhere, do anything, and the only person who can stop you is yourself. Find out what you need, and then pay the price. Go for it. It doesn't matter how many people know you; it only matters how useful you are to them. It doesn't matter how big your product is; it only matters how it cooperates with others.

The car we drive is very useful, but we don't pay attention to the first person who thought of it. The history of the car has become meaningless. The car cannot start without gas in the tank, and the gas is useless without an engine. You drive your car to the garage, buy fuel, and then drive to another place. The gas is useful; the car cannot start until there's gas in it. This requires cooperation. Everything needs another thing in order to achieve one goal. Each one of us must do his work in order for the world to run. That's why you don't have to neglect your work. You have a way of seeing things that I don't; you have a way of doing things that I don't.

If we join our hands together, nothing will be impossible in this world. Respect your time and don't quit, because you don't know if you've arrived. Remember that water can only boil at one hundred degree Celsius. If you get all the way to ninety-nine degrees, you'll have to get one degree warmer in order to make it. Don't say that you got tired, otherwise you will have run your course in vain.

Look where you've come from and the time you've spent. Don't give up. You are a permanent loser when you decide to give up. Go for it! You're about to see the goal. Until you make your goal happen, be quiet and don't quit. It's not over until it's over.

I NEED YOUR BRAIN

Before a person asks anything from a computer, he or she must make sure the information already exists inside the computer. A computer will never give you anything new. If you ask your computer to reveal your dreams this coming night, it will tell you, "You're out of your mind." You have asked the wrong question. Why? Because none of this information has been registered. But if you ask the computer what day of the week fell on January 1, 2000? It will tell you that it was a Saturday.

Human brains act like computers. What the eyes see and the ears hear make the heart believe and the mouth speak—and then comes action. If I'm jealous of anything you have, it's the potential within you. Please, I need it. Don't hold it until it expires. Give it away, do something with it, let it go. Even though the computer is compared to the human brain, the computer is still one of the human brain's creations. A human brain creates a computer, but a computer can never create a man.

A computer only has the capacity to operate on the level of the information you give it in advance. It has no emotion. If two persons ask the same question to a computer, it will give the same answer. But according to the human brain, based on the matter of emotion, a person can give different answers to the same question.

For instance, if a computer directs a weapon to shoot anybody standing at your door, it will shoot you if you make the mistake of standing at that door. You won't be surprised, but your neighbour will be; she'll be the one to explain your story after you're gone. But if you give a gun to a security guard and ask him to kill those who prowl around your house at night, nothing will happen to you, because the security guard knows that he's supposed to protect you. Computers help a lot, but the brain thinks more. That's why the computer has been not only created by the human brain, but also manufactured by the human hand.

The essence of being motivated is to know where you're going and that you're on the right track with a compelling desire to get there. As we know, satisfaction creates motivation, and motivation increases satisfaction. When you take time achieving your goal, remember this: your goal or dream isn't community property.

Your dream is yours. That's why you are who you are and have the capacity you have, and also why you have the time you've been given to achieve your goal. Act as though the only result the world is waiting for is yours. Act as if you were locked in a room with an explosive device telling you that it will blow up in few minutes. Look around and see that there's nobody else but you. All the doors are locked. Nobody is watching. The only person who needs to be rescued is you, and the one who must intervene is you alone.

In a situation like this, you *will* do something. Why? Because pressure motivates you, gives you a reason to act. Without it, nothing can get done. Accept pressure; it puts you in a position to prepare for opportunity.

When preparation meets opportunity, there's often an explosion. We used to see people with opportunity but no preparation. When pressure comes, you must do something. You must link pain to your life's goal. Your goals demand pressure, and pressure can be a personal catalyst. All goals face both opportunity and opposition, and both start within us. If we had the chance to perceive what God is waiting for us to fulfill, and the capacity He has given us to make it happen, we wouldn't miss a single opportunity.

Every time we feel like we're down to nothing, God is up to something. Don't live by mistake. The time you have mustn't be taken for granted, because there is a purpose for it. Use time creatively, and don't leave this world without abandoning what it requires of you.

What a pity it is to die with food while people are starving to death. Remember that the world is watching you. It won't stop without you, but it will step with you. There's something in this world only you can discover, only you can do, and only you can make. Others might be able to do it, but only you have such perfection to accomplish it. That's why the entire world is waiting on you.

Take time to discover it and start doing it. When you motivate yourself, you set yourself apart from the crowd. You come to understand yourself and others much better. Your actions are consistent, your perception is sharpened, and your decisions are sound. Your creative sense improves daily. You begin to lay out plans, anticipate obstacles, generate target dates, and take action on your wants, needs, and desires.

Your motivation is a desire held in expectation with the belief that it will be realized. Your ability to believe it determines your ability to receive it. This is the time to use the unlimited potential you possess.

The fact is that the world is overflowing with abundance, but very few people trust their potential. How in the world can someone else trust you if you don't first trust yourself? Do you know that your brain controls the function of more than two hundred bones, six hundred muscles, and twenty kilometres of ducts and respiratory glands? It regulates the heart in pumping seven tons of blood every twenty-four hours and controls the processing of eight thousand litres of air daily. Isn't that amazing? God created a brain within you which has time to fulfill its purposes, but you who possess it don't have the time to believe it.

We tend to take for granted the abundance that we produce. If we accept the perceived self-limiting restrictions that bad conditioning has placed upon us, how will we expect to achieve anything? We always receive in accordance with what we expect. Expect more, receive more; expect little, receive little.

Men build machines that fly, swim, and move mountains. We build all sorts of appliances, but we build our lives on stupidity. Your potential is unlimited until you place limits upon yourself. A measure of your success is what you are now compared to what you can become. Success always involves progress, growth, movement, action, change, risk, and love.

TAKE A RISK SOMETIMES

G oal-setting creates a climate of growth and change which inevitably produces an inspirational discontent with the way things are. Your imagination, creativity, and potential for success only become useful when you put them to work.

As the saying goes, no pain, no gain. If you choose to live without risk, you'll achieve no progress, create no inventions, make no discoveries. Risk requires courage, because without courage no risk will be taken. The refusal of risk sets up the most foolish risk ever taken, ironically, and also may create the possibility of you missing the opportunity to fulfill your dreams. Achievement is a direct consequence of striving for clearly defined goals. In war, the moment you rest, the enemy has the opportunity to conquer your land. Write down your goals before forsaking them in the shuffle and excitement of new decisions, new problems, or new challenges. Written goals will help you conserve time and energy, keeping you on track to progress and eliminate outside distractions.

Circumstances exist not in the environment we're in, but within ourselves. Divide each obstacle into small obstacles, then face one small obstacle at a time. For instance, if you can't pick up one heavy stone, what should you do? Divide it into small pieces, then handle them one by one.

After setting goals, you must take time to plan which strategy is best. You might be passionate about helping the world, but without a plan you'll accomplish nothing. Your goals need a map. The map will show you where you are and where you're going.

The map to achieving your goals must be as explicit and clear as possible, with as much detail packed into it as you can manage. If you fail to plan, you already plan to fail. Spend more time on drawing the map to form a clear picture of your destination, then ask yourself these basic questions—why? where? which? what? who? and when?

For example:

Why am I going?
Where am I going?
Which way will I use to get there?
What do I need?
Who do I need?
When this must happen?

Answer these questions according to the goal set before you. If you cannot see it in your mind, you're probably not going to see it with your eyes. Take the time to dream, to plan your goal and be able to see the end of your mission.

If you don't see the end, don't start. You need to be aware of the situation you'll encounter. Don't assume. Don't guess. Don't try to be a magician. Know what's ahead of you. Study and ask questions so you'll have enough information concerning the particular project you face. If you want to build a tower, count the cost first, as Luke 14:28 says.

Remember that a dog chasing an elephant is just having fun. My mother drummed this adage into my head ever since I was seven years old. Doing things without a plan is like a medical student trying to perform an operation after even reading a book about it.

A pilot is supposed to know his departure point and destination. In the same way, you must know the beginning and the end of your mission. If you know where you're going, you'll also know which way will take you there. If you don't know where you're going, any way will take you there. At that point, it's useless to talk about time, because it could take you a lifetime.

A civil engineer will never start a building unless he sees the plan. When you have a plan, you save time and energy. Don't start anything unless you see the end. See the end, then back up to the beginning. Plan your task ahead of time.

Time is so important, much more powerful than we have ever considered. That's why we take it for granted. But if we really get the revelation of time's power, it will revolt us at the point of beginning to wonder about the reason we're living the way we are. We'll always tackle the "why" before the "how," and then our actions will have purpose.

Emergency Time

The actions you take in desperate situation must take priority over your expectation of somebody else's assistance. Others will never sense what you sense; they will never see exactly what you see.

When my father passed away, I was twenty-two years old in the Congo. He collapsed one morning, and I was the only boy in the house at the time. We didn't have a car to bring him to the hospital, nor a telephone to call somebody.

One neighbour had seen our frustration and called someone with a car. This guy picked us up and dropped me and my father at the hospital. In my head, I was thinking, *What luck!* That's when I saw the sign that read: "Emergency." With my father in my hands, we approached the door and started knocking. I saw doctors inside through the glass. They acted as if they didn't see us; they ignored us. I thought to myself, *Maybe they don't understand.* So I tried to show them my father, who was in very bad shape.

One assistant came and looked at me. Without opening the door, he gestured to me with his hands. I thought, *My goodness, why this place called "Emergency"? Even if they don't understand what I'm saying, they can at least see what's going on.* Finally, I said, "Okay, let's go where they want us to go."

I took my father again into my hands and walked with him to another part of the hospital. My father couldn't realize what was going on, as he was unconscious. We had arrived at the hospital at 7:30 a.m., but got assisted around 10:45. I was more sick and tired than my father. I had an emergency case, but I didn't know that the doctor had his, too. A few weeks later, my father succumbed to diabetes.

I came to realize that "emergency" isn't just a word on a hospital sign; it's what you have to do in times of need before you think about getting assistance from others. The only thing I know is this: if you call for an ambulance and a pizza at the same time, the pizza will come first. In fact, only once you're on your way to the rubbish can to throw away the box will the ambulance arrive.

There are people who haven't been through tough situations. It's hard to comprehend what you've never seen or experienced.

A child once asked his father, "Daddy, what does it mean to be hungry?"

His father was very shocked. "Son, we're going for a ride."

They hadn't eaten any breakfast yet, which the father had done on purpose.

In the car, they rolled along for six hours nonstop. Then the child said, "Daddy, can you stop and buy me some chocolate?"

"Son, we're about to reach the place. Just wait a little longer."

He drove another two hours. After a while, the child didn't say anything, but he did start to cry.

The father stopped the car. "What's going on, son?"

"Daddy, I want to eat something."

"Now you've got it," the father said. "What you feel is called hunger. You are hungry. I wanted you, my son, to find it by yourself so you would never forget it."

If you've ever pleaded for the great God to end your life because you just couldn't seem to reach the other side, you know what I'm talking about. If you've walked fifteen kilometres every day for several years just to get to school and back, you know what I'm talking about. If you've endured working for an unmerciful boss so that your children won't lack bread on the table, you know what I'm talking about.

If you've worked for years in order to accumulate everything you need in life—such as a house, cars, and much more—only to lose it all to a sudden hurricane or flood, leaving you with nothing but a cell phone in your hand, you know what I'm talking about. If you've spent three days in the month of January without electricity in Canada, you know what I'm talking about. If you've spent a week on an airport bench because you couldn't afford a hotel room, you know what I'm talking about.

If you've been divorced not because you lack love but because you're broke, you know what I'm talking about. If you've ever denied yourself just so you could be accepted by others, you know what I'm talking about. If you've sold your house to get into a business that went bankrupt, you know what I'm talking about. If you've slept with money in your pocket and woke up with change and asked yourself how in the world this could be, you know what I'm talking about.

If you've been refused admittance in certain countries because you're suspected of not being yourself, you know what I'm talking about. If you've lost your self-esteem just by being betrayed, you know what I'm talking about. If you've had to sleep four siblings on the same double bed for a month, you know what I'm talking about. If you've sold your blood so you could have food on the table, you know what I'm talking about.

If you've ever entered into a prayer and fasted for your husband so he could be fired from work because you're sick and tired of him, you know what I'm talking about. If you've paid a dowry for a girl only to find out that she already got married to another man, you know what I'm talking about. If your phone call was answered by a romantic rival when you called your fiancé, you know what I'm talking about.

If you've watched as a member of your family died in your arms, wishing you could do something but were unable to change the situation, you know what I'm talking about.

You may not identify with all these tragic situations. Nevertheless, if you've experienced any tragedies in life that left you in a dilemma where you had to choose not between "good" and "bad," but between "bad" and "worse," I'm talking to you.

EXPECT OPPOSITION IN LIFE

D on't be affected by other people's opinion of you. It doesn't matter who you are, your position, or your career. It doesn't even matter how good you can be to others. You may have the most passionate heart, able to carry the entire world in you. There will always be somebody who opposes you.

We can look back in the history of humanity to see that there has never been such thing as a human being who has unanimously gained the entire population's approval. In countries under dictatorship, people have to fake their emotions and actions because they don't want to be put to jail or have some kind of disciplinary action taken against them. These people will fake their actions to accommodate the rule of law, even though they totally disagree with it.

You can perform nothing but kind and good actions, and yet opposition is inevitable. It doesn't matter who you are; you just have to know that some people will embrace you and others will reject you. That's the way it is.

Consider the three SW's: some will, some won't, so what?

When President Clinton was in power of the U.S., people claimed he was the antichrist. It was the same story with President George W. Bush, and the same is true with President Obama. Some celebrate him, yet others are busy spreading rumours.

What can we do? We don't have to wait on everyone's approval. Do what you know is right. Never let the intimidation of opposition paralyze you, because somebody will always disapprove of you. Sometimes you'll find that people hate you for no reason at all.

So, what are you going to do? Dig your own tomb and bury yourself? Absolutely not! This is part of life. You have to deal with it. Be not a victim. If you aren't careful, people will impose on you how you're supposed to feel about any given situation, even when you may feel differently. Consider opposition as a step toward your destiny. Whenever you encounter opposition, it's just a sign telling you that you need to shoot high.

Michael Jordan was once prohibited from playing basketball. Can you imagine? Who in the world would have the guts to stop Jordan from playing basketball now? He faced opposition, but Jordan took it as a step toward his destiny; he went on training hard and eventually became among the greatest—if not the greatest—basketball player of all time.

You need to consider opposition as a step, not a stop, toward your destiny.

Can I Help You?

I'm sure many of us are familiar with these four words: "Can I help you?" We've heard them in different ways, at different places, at different moments, and from different people.

This question has been asked of us all our lives, most of the time with an attitude behind it. But if asked from the bottom of one's heart, it's a gentle and loving question with which to start a day. You don't want to start a day by thinking, *What can I get today? Who's going to help me?* Those are selfish questions.

You rather have to ask yourself these questions: *What can I give today? Who can I help? Who can I encourage?* We have a tendency to expose our problems to others. I think we need to take time also to listen to others. If we do, we'll surely discover that people around us have more problems than we. Moreover, when you realize that others have more problem than you, the next thing you do is forget your own problems and start helping others.

This world is full of hurting people. If you had the chance, conduct a survey of your neighbourhood. Give everyone a piece of paper and pen and ask them to list all the problems that bother them. You'll end up with a lot of papers filled with writing.

Everybody on earth has problems. When we reach out to others, we discover that the one we wanted to help is now helping us. You may be struggling with something I consider a piece of cake, and I may be in a nightmare which to you is laughably easy.

Let's take a practical example. If you look at the production line in an automobile factor, you'd be amazed. Every vehicle produced is touched by more than 180 employees. These 180 employees each perform a specific task. Every one is qualified to do one thing, but when the car comes together it makes for a single finished product. One person may not know how to fix a tire, but he could be a genius with sound systems. What if the genius in sound systems looked down on the tire guy and said, "I'm better than you"? Well, a car may have the best sound system ever, but without tires it won't go anywhere.

Big companies understand this. They hire different people and put them together to work as a team. I bring what I know, you bring what you know, and a third person brings what they know. At the end of the day, we make a finished product.

Whatever you're thinking about right now is more than a mere thought. It's not in you by accident. There's a meaning for it. Put your thoughts on paper, ask questions, and discuss them with others. Some people will know things you don't, and others will want to know what you know. As a matter of fact, somebody told you everything you know today, either in school, through parents, friends, and media, or by reading a book.

You may have the solution to the thing I'm struggling with, and I may have the solution to what you're struggling with. I know what you don't know, and you know what I don't know. Guess what? If you hide from me what you know I need, and I hide from you what I know you need, we'll have unresolved problems for the rest of our lives.

Can I help you? Ask this of someone on the street today. This is how you can reach out to others. Before you know it, somebody else will be able to reach out to you.

Be Away from Complainers

We need to identify the people who complain about everything in life, most of the time for no reason at all. It is said that a human being has sixty thousand thoughts every single day. Eighty percent of these thoughts repeat themselves from day to day, and ninety percent are negative. We are bombarded by negative thoughts constantly. As if that wasn't enough, you sit and listen to complainers all the time. We are exposed to the attack of negative thoughts. That's a fact. But we can do something to prevent ourselves from drowning.

If you want to have something to complain about, just open your eyes and ears for a minute. There is, and there will always be, something to complain about. It's up to us to say, "Even if I complain, it won't help." Instead of complaining about what's wrong, consider one right thing you can be grateful for. Just as there's always something to complain about, there's always something to be grateful for as well.

One day, as I was doing my weekly grocery shopping, I picked up everything I needed and went to the counter.

There I was at the checkout, in front of a beautiful young girl. I could see that she was a complainer.

While she was passing my items through the scanner, I asked her how she was doing. It was like she had been waiting for that moment to release what was in her heart. After all, when the car is ready to go, the only thing it's waiting for is to be put in gear.

"I hate my life," she said to me.

"Well, I asked you how you're doing today. That's it."

Again she said, "I hate my life."

I looked at her. "You hate your life, but I can assure you right now there's somebody in a desperate situation, somebody who's going to die, who's praying to God so he can have the life you hate."

She stood speechless as I walked out.

Every day I go to that store, I see that girl. I can see a change in her. There's a smile on her face as she wishes me good morning. I believe she got the message.

Who in the world would want to live with a complaining co-worker, friend, husband, or wife? Proverbs 21:9 says it this way:

It is better to dwell in a corner of the housetop [on the flat oriental roof, exposed to all kinds of weather] than in a house shared with a nagging, quarrelsome, and faultfinding woman.

According to science, you can catch a bad habit the same way you catch a cold. That's why we need to be away from complainers. By being close to a complaining person, it won't take long for you to be like them. As the saying goes, we become exactly like who we spend time with. Who do you spend your days with?

Adjust Yourself

If you've been a driver, you may agree that while you're driving uphill in a car—especially one with a manual transmission—you need to change gears in order to reach the top of the hill. Let's say that you start the car and put it into first gear, then second, and then third. If you're facing the hill, it would be wise to downshift to the second or the first, or else you won't make it.

After playing a bit of golf, I decided that I'd never forget the most stressful moment in the game: how to get the ball out of the bunker. You probably know what a bunker is, but just in case you don't, it's a hazard with lots of sand in it. You have to avoid it in order to reach the green. Once the ball hits the sand, it becomes a challenge to get it out. A golfer can't panic, for he has a variety of clubs at his disposal. For example, if his ball falls into a bunker, it would be useless to play with a putter, nor a hybrid, and much less a driver. He must use a sand wedge. He'll have to adjust by using the right club. Without adjustment, his shot won't be effective.

It's the same in life. We need to know how to adjust. Never be a victim of circumstances. You can adjust or relocate, but never say you had no choice. You always have choices.

I read that Sally Kristen Ride was a professional tennis player who couldn't perform very well. Most of us would simply try harder, but not Sally. She decided to enroll at Stanford University. At the age of twenty-seven, with a Bachelor of Arts, a Bachelor of Science, a master's degree, and a Ph.D., she started looking for postdoctoral work in astrophysics. That's when she read about NASA's call for astronauts in the Stanford University paper. More than eight thousand men and women applied to the space program that year. Only thirty-five were accepted, and only six of these were women. One was Sally Ride.

After joining NASA in 1977, Ride underwent extensive training that included parachute jumping, water survival, gravity and weight training, and radio communications. In 1983, Dr. Ride became the first American woman in space.

She made adjustments. You don't have to force yourself into becoming something you're not. You are equipped with whatever you need in order to perform in a certain domain. It will never be a surprise to you, because you know what you're capable of. So, adjust to that and be yourself.

BE WHO YOU ARE

You can't perform to your fullest capacity by trying to be me. It's easier and more natural for you to be yourself than trying to be somebody else.

Can you imagine for a second what it would be like to see Michael Jordan racing in Formula One? He could do it. I've seen him on TV saying that he would never claim he couldn't do something without trying it first. Not only is he known worldwide to be among the greatest basketball players of all time, but he performs easily and naturally in basketball.

Be who you are. You have no competitor in your category, because you're unique. Why then are you trying so hard to be somebody else? Tavis Smiley once said that you might as well be yourself, because everybody else has already been taken. This means that everyone else you are forcefully trying to be has already been taken, but the only one who's available for you to be is you. God created you as an original man or woman, so why would you want to die a copy of somebody else? Are you saying that God made a mistake by creating you? He never makes mistakes. In fact, when He finished manufacturing you,

He said to Himself, "This is what I wanted." If God wanted you tall, you would have been tall. If He wanted you short, you would have been short. If He wanted you white, you would have been white. If He wanted you black, you would have been black.

The reason you are the way you are is that you're a complete package created by God Himself, with every necessary thing in it, to perform and excel to the limit. Quit trying so hard to be who you're not and start enjoying who you are.

You are equipped to excel in life. There's no doubt about it. The reason you'll excel is that you're alive. If you have the breath of life, it's enough for you to do what you're called to do. You may ask, "How is it to be, with the situation I'm in?" If you ever try to complain about anything, I dare you to google this name: Nick Vujicic. Take some time to watch this man. If you google him, you'll agree that you have all it takes to succeed. As you can see, Nick is not imitating anybody. No, he's just living as Nick is supposed to live. Instead of complaining about what he doesn't have, he rather enjoys who he is and performs to the fullest.

You need to be who you are to stay on track. A car, for example, has been invented to drive on solid ground. What would happen if I put my car on the river and expected it to perform as a boat? I would destroy it, by the simple fact that it hasn't been invented to travel on water. When a manufacturer makes a car, he puts specific things into that car that will never be useful elsewhere but on the ground. He also puts in place certain laws on which the car must operate. In other words, using your car on the water would be called *abuse*—which means "abnormal use."

The same principle applies to us. As human beings, when we try to be somebody else, we work hard only to copy another person, forgetting that we are originals.

Go to any mall and sit down someplace where you're able to see the flow of the crowd. You'll notice one thing: everybody comes for a specific length of time, to a specific place, to do or buy a specific thing. In fact, if you stay in the mall long enough, such as after 10:00 p.m., you'll be the only one left. Why? Because everyone came with a purpose, for a limited time. Let's say you know the reason you went to the mall and you happen to have an encounter with one of your friends. Your friend may ask you to go here or there, which wasn't in your schedule. This means your friend took you off-track; he's on-track, because he's going where he's supposed to go. But he took you with him on his schedule. We do that in life. We often forget what we've been created to do, and end up doing what we see other people do.

Just as we see people walking around the mall to a specific place, for a specific time, to do or buy a specific thing, God created each of us to live on this earth for a specific length of time, at a specific place, for a specific reason or mission. Every time you try to imitate others, you get yourself off-track. To get back on-track, you have to be yourself.

Don't allow yourself to be a copy of another individual. You are an original, so act like it. Live like it. When you imitate others, you'll certainly limit yourself, because imitation is nothing but limitation.

FIRST IMPRESSION

D on't sell yourself short, because you're worth more. How do you present yourself, especially when you have to be at a place where other people will observe or judge you? Like going to a job interview or going on first date? Remember this: in life, you'll never have a second chance to make a first impression.

Who in the world would want to hire a person in customer service who's dressed in blue jeans and white t-shirt with oil all over it? If I was the employer, I'd think, *This is what you'll bring to my company?* I don't care how smart you might be. The reality is that you may be a genius, but if you go to an interview looking like you just came from the pit of hell, you'll struggle to get hired. As a matter of fact, it's not always the aptitude, but the attitude that determines someone's altitude.

Most of the time we buy things, we don't do it because we need them but because they look good. Here's the test. Go into your closet and look around. You'll find some clothes you bought a year ago but haven't had a chance to wear yet. Why? The answer: because they looked good in the shop. You really didn't *need* them. And that was only in the closet!

We're attracted by good appearances. It's in our nature. I'm not saying we have to go after any good appearance we see, but it's easy to grasp the quality of something—or someone—by its appearance.

If you watched the 2012 American presidential debates, you might have noticed something important. Governor Romney had a chance to win the election, but every time he had to present his plan, even though it may have been brilliant, he would say, "This is what I'll do *if* I'm elected president." Obama, on his turn, said, "This is what I'll do *as* the president."

I hope you see the difference. Who are you going to vote for—the one who knows he's the president, or the one who wishes to become one? You'll likely vote for the one who is confident of himself. I'm sure people were saying, "This guy isn't even sure if he'll be the president." There was a lack of confidence. Romney's plan may have been better than Obama's, but he appeared uncertain. Even if you have nothing much to say, your appearance, confidence, and attitude speaks on your behalf.

Several months before that election, at the London Olympics, I saw a young man from Jamaica named Usain Bolt. This young man was called the fastest man on earth because he was the first to cross the finish line—in 9.36 seconds. That was a record time on the men's one-hundred-metre dash. Again, he won the men's four-hundred-meter race. As if that wasn't enough, four years earlier, at the Beijing Olympics in 2008, he was also the first to cross the line. The guy was awarded the athlete of the year in 2012.

At the starting point, while the runners were getting ready to run, you could guess that Bolt would get the gold medal. How could you tell? You just had to look at his attitude. He was neither frustrated nor confused; he was as calm as could be.

What impression are you presenting? Especially when it's the first one?

ACCEPT CHANGE

The only constant and inevitable thing in life is change. We must accept it if we intend to progress to the next level. We barely accept change, because when we get used to something, it becomes familiar and difficult to interrupt. Refusing change is like a baby saying, "I want to remain a baby for all time."

We've all been babies, but we had to grow up when the time came. We had to feed ourselves. In effect, we had to say, "I don't need milk anymore. I need solid food, because I'm no longer a baby; I'm a grown-up person." That's change.

In fact, we *can* refuse change. Whether we like it or not, though, change will affect us. I've heard that when cars first became available in the early 1900s, some people were sure they were a fad. They believed the horse and buggy would forever be part of their lives. As an elderly American citizen once said, "We either had to move with modern times or get out of the street." Can you imagine what a horse and buggy would be like on the freeway nowadays? We don't ignore the importance and necessity of horses, but we realize that there's no place for a horse on the freeway.

Before 1990, I wrote letters to some of my correspondents around the world. It would take at least forty-five days for my letter to travel from Africa to Europe, and then from Europe to Africa. In other words, every time I sent a letter, I'd have to wait a month and a half to get a reply or answer.

That was back then, but what about today? Being in Canada, if I want to send a letter to my brother in Africa, I'll send him an email. He'll get it right away. And that's not all. I can also text him. I can go even further and chat with him on Skype. Why should I wait forty-five days? Give me a break.

When IBM produced the first computer in 1960, it was a huge computer whose volume could be compared to the size of the average bedroom. Today, I carry that same amount of power right in my pocket. It's called a smartphone. The old times are over and change has come.

Being a writer, I used to walk with a pen and notebook. I was unable to carry a dictionary, so most of the time I would refrain from leaving the house. I wanted to make sure I had all my tools when an idea came to mind. I'm not obligated to be home anymore in order to write. My creativity increases when I unlock myself from my room.

As a matter of fact, today I don't need to carry all the tools from my office to be able to write. One thing is enough for me: my phone. With my phone, I don't need a pen, a notebook, or a dictionary... because everything I need—or will ever need—is in the phone.

Change has come. We have to take with us what was useful from the past so we can embrace the twenty-first century. Change has come not to surprise us but to take us to the next level.

Why Are We Running?

We're running so fast that most of the time we don't even know where we're headed. As a matter of fact, we bypass other people without looking at them. The reason for all this, I guess, is that we want to be the first ones to get "there." What is "there"? I don't know. There's no way to define it.

We sometimes forget that those we pay less attention to in life might be our gatekeepers. Life isn't about the destination. Joel Osteen once said that it's about how we live along the way. My question is, why are we running? There are those who run from something, while others run toward something. In other words, some run free while others run scared. Here comes the question again: why are you running?

Talk show host Steve Harvey's father once said to him, "My son, there is a lion in the jungle, and the lion said, 'Every morning when I get up, I have to run, otherwise I will starve to death.' On the other side of the jungle, there's a gazelle who said, 'Every morning, I have to run, otherwise I'll be the prey to the lion.'" The conclusion is this: every morning when you wake up, it doesn't matter who you are; you must start running.

We run so fast and are so goal-oriented that we don't even consider others. But where are we headed and why are we running? Have you ever stopped running and asked yourself this question? We make the mistake of considering a goal to be more important than the human being on the way to our goal. Whenever your goal becomes more important than your spouse or your kids, check again. It might be the wrong goal, or maybe you have the wrong priorities in life.

One morning, I drove to work with a friend. A few minutes before reaching the company, we perceived a stopped vehicle in front of us. We had no idea what was wrong; we didn't see anybody nearby. I said to my friend that it was very dangerous to stop on the freeway. We passed by and went on. While we were busy working later, one of my co-workers leaned over to me and said, "Cletous, do you know what happened this morning?"

"Tell me," I said.

"Apparently, a guy on the freeway got hit by a car."

When I heard that, I immediately realized that it could have been the guy from the stopped car I saw. I said to myself, *If only somebody had been willing to stop and give the guy a ride, nothing worse might have happened.*

Here's what happened. He was driving with a passenger when the vehicle broke down. They got out of the car and started walking so they could get to work, which was just a half-mile away. Another person who worked at the same company accidentally hit one of them, and the one who was hit gave up his last breath on the spot.

Perhaps this sad situation occurred because we're all running. We run so fast and carelessly. What is happening on the way? It's common to say, "I don't care. That's his problem. What does it have to do with me?" These are self-centred words, and we need to get rid of them.

How would you feel if you had everything you needed in this world—I mean everything—but then you looked around and saw that there was nobody but yourself? Imagine you had the entire world with everything in it, but you were alone. I assure you that you would be a miserable, bored wretch. Our possessions only make sense if there are people around us. Don't take those people for granted. Enjoy them and acknowledge them, because they're part of you. Help them when they need you. They're important to the world, and to you as well.

If we took a moment to think, we'd realize that we face more struggles today because we act like we're in competition with everyone else. We all do what it takes to achieve our goals, even if it ends another person's life. We forget that there should be more cooperation than competition. It's sad to realize that we're in an unending race, trying to perform to the fullest so the world will know who we really are.

I'm here to let you know that we're not in competition. Look at your neighbour not as a rival to compete with but as someone to complete you.

At the Paralympics in 1970, several competitors lined up their wheelchairs at the starting line of a race. After they started, one of them fell out of his chair, blocking some of the others' paths. A couple of seconds later, this accident caused a few more athletes to fall out. Now, the one who was leading realized that something was wrong, so he stopped. The one after him stopped, too. Everybody stopped. Those who were ready to run went back and started picking up or lifting the fallen ones off the track.

You know what they did? They started the race again, this time not competing but rather completing one another to make sure they all arrived together at the finish line hand-in-hand. Never before had such love been displayed in the entire history of the Paralympic—not before, and certainly not since.

Happiness from Within

We have a tendency to condition happiness by what's happening out in the world. We say things like "I'll be happy when this is gone" or "I'll be happy when I get that." Some people go even further by saying, "I'll be happy when my kids go to college," but after they're in college they say, "I'll be happy when they graduate from college." Whenever your happiness becomes conditional on external circumstances, you'll live a miserable life. Why? Circumstances can change at any time. People can leave you when you least expect it.

There are those who say, "I'll be happy when I purchase my home." After they get the home, they say, "I'll be happy once I sell my house." There are still some who say, "I'll be happy when I get married," but they ignore all those people who say, "I'll be happy if I get a divorce." There's no such thing as "I'll be happy when..." You can be happy right where you are now; it depends on your decision.

If your happiness comes from things and people, you'll always suffer the consequences of the environment around you. It's preferable to become the one deciding whether or not you want to be happy.

I once read a book called *Every Day a Friday*, by Joel Osteen.[2] This book grabbed my attention. Osteen writes about everyday life, about the way we react to certain situations, about what motivates us, and also about how we think the only day of the week on which to be happy at work is Friday. That's not true. We make it a reality, then start believing it has to be that way.

I guess this is because we intend for happiness to come from what we see, what we touch, and how we feel. In other words, we want happiness to come from what we experience through our senses instead of from within. This isn't an example of extroverts versus introverts. It goes far beyond that. If we think we have to accomplish this or that for us to be happy, what then will we say about those who have already done what we're trying to do but aren't happy at all?

Happiness is your decision, not what happens to you. That means you have a role to play in being happy. Don't let the circumstances of life decide for you. Nevertheless, no one ignores the reality that there are people who have everything they could possibly need or want but still aren't happy. This makes it obvious that things aren't the source of happiness. Rather, happiness comes from within. In the same way that we can see individuals with almost everything they need still be miserable, we also see those who have almost nothing and yet are happy as can be.

The best example of a person who has nothing within him but happiness is a young man I mentioned

---

2 Joel Osteen, *Every Day a Friday* (Nashville, TN: FaithWords, 2011).

earlier—Nick Vujicic. I asked you to google him. I hope you did. You see, Nick has neither arms nor legs, but he is fulfilling his mission to the fullest. More importantly, you never see him unhappy, while the majority of people have it all and are still unhappy.

We don't have to have everything we want or need to live happily, because happiness is a decision within our reach.

ESCAPE FROM IGNORANCE

When I was a child, we lived in a neighbourhood which was considered the lowest of the lower classes. We didn't even know we were poor, because everybody around us lived like us. There was no comparison, no reference at all. We thought everyone in that place was normal, until one day our father decided that we should move to a middle-class area. That's when I started seeing things I had never seen before.

My elder brothers told me that our father had lived a good life long before, but by the time I was born something really bad had happened to the family. In 1962, my father bought a brand-new minivan and used it to taxi people between the cities of Lubumbashi and Likasi. Unfortunately, my father happened to hire a bad driver; from his name, you could tell something was wrong. He was called Mutombo le Fou—in other words, Mutombo the Mad.

Mutombo had a friend who also drove the same type of minivan, and the two drivers would play crazy games on the road, and always with passengers aboard. When they had to cross one another on the road, they would signal one another; after one driver signalled, the other would signal back as a response to confirm that it was his friend. After a successful exchange of signals, the driver on the left-hand side would go to the right, and the one on the right would go to the left. In other words, they switched sides. They had practiced this trick a couple of times without any trouble.

No passenger seemed to have a problem with it. Or if they did, they didn't say anything. Who was one to correct Mutombo le Fou?

One day, our driver was on the road from Likasi to Lubumbashi. While traveling at a very high speed, he noticed a minivan approaching from the opposite direction. He thought it was his friend, so he signalled and the other driver signalled back. Mutombo was now a hundred percent sure it was his friend. On cue, he switched sides, as he normally did, expecting the other driver to do the same.

It wasn't his friend.

Neither driver knew what to do next at this point, so they ended up in a dramatic collision. There were more than ten passengers in each minivan, and every one died on the spot—including my own uncle. This tragic event left my entire family in crisis.

Many years later, after our family moved into the middle-class neighbourhood, we still ate just one meal a day. My new friends, however, ate three meals a day—including breakfast. I was dumbfounded and said to myself, *Wait a second... am I dreaming?* We had to walk to school, seven miles each way, but my friends rode the bus. We had to drink water straight from the tap under the burning sun, while our neighbours drank fresh water from the fridge. For us to have fun, we had to play in the mud; our friends had all kind of toys. We had to wear the same clothes for a week. When they got dirty, we'd wash them during the night and hang them to the drier rope so we could wear them in the morning. Our friends would change clothes every single day! Our mother had to use charcoal in the kitchen when she cooked; our friends had stoves and ovens in their kitchens. Our uncles and aunties told us bedtime stories before going to sleep, because we couldn't afford any other entertainment. Our friends had the privilege of watching TV. We used to put our plates and food on the floor while eating, but our neighbours ate at the table.

In this new city, everybody had a family name except us. When I say "name," I don't mean just the family name one might find on a passport. A name included what one's father and mother did for a living, or perhaps it described their possessions. That's how we were able to recognize the other families in this new city. All our friends had names because they were well-known, but we were nobodies who had come from a lower class. Thus we were pushed to work hard, not to create a family name but to create an individual name for each of us. We did it.

I was grateful to be in the new neighbourhood, because it's where I at last realized how broke we were. I was unable to see the truth at our first home for the simple fact that everybody around us lived exactly the same. How do you know what you're missing if you've never seen it before? You have to perceive a thing before you can realize you lack it. The best I could see as a child was that everyone ate just one meal per day; therefore it became the standard, the definition of normal.

This conception was engraved in my subconscious until the day our father forcefully moved us from that remote and poor neighbourhood to one where we could see how other people lived. Just seeing our friends have breakfast, lunch, and dinner kindled a revolution inside us. We began to say to one another, "There's something missing; there's something better than what we actually know."

Step by step, we interacted with our friends to learn. I'm grateful for my father; had he not been so bold and courageous, we wouldn't be where we are today. I remember when he first told us that we were moving—the very next day! No one agreed to go. We thought he had lost his mind. What was going on? Where were we going, and why? But my father saw something we didn't, for he had experienced that life before. Perhaps if he had tried to negotiate with us, none of us would have gone. So he had to take us by force.

Dear friends, what you don't know will kill you. In other words, ignorance is as venomous as a snake. We have to flee from it. There are thousands upon thousands of new things to discover.

You're trapped by what you ignore. You're limited and can rise only to the level of your knowledge. The difference between you and somebody who seems to be higher than you has nothing to do with their possessions. Before we moved to the new town, we didn't know what poverty meant. As soon as we got there, we discovered that we were poor. We took a step forward, eventually coming out of that miserable situation.

You may say that it's better not to know better, but that's just an excuse for ignorance. Ignorance is not, and never will be, an excuse to avoid death. Hosea 4:6 says,

"My people are destroyed for lack of knowledge." That comes straight from God! As we realize that what's killing us is what we don't know, let us inform ourselves and learn everything we can to help us escape ignorance.

BETTER THAN THIS

We've probably all heard someone say, "Just get the job done." Does it matter *how* the job is done? It's not about doing things correctly, but doing the correct things. You can do a wrong thing correctly, so it's really not about doing things correctly. Remember that the best is the enemy of the good. Who wants to help his peer when he barely has enough? If you have more than enough, it will be natural for you to help. Nobody will push you to give, and so you'll do it willingly.

Life can feel routine. We may start believing that our current circumstances are merely the way things are, and that they will always be that way. What a way to look at life! Think about this for a second. You are born, and then you go to kindergarten, elementary school, junior high, high school, and college or university. You take a break for a month or two, and then you get a job. After that, you take on a mortgage. You work your entire life only to find out that you can't finish paying the mortgage, so you leave it to your children after you die. Your children take over and do the same as you. There's got to be a better way. We're stuck, because we don't use our

God-given potential to the fullest to create things and think big.

Sometimes our degrees put limits on us. Your degree may act as your own tomb; when you have a certain degree, the only thing that comes to your mind is your target job. With this mindset, you won't be able to see any higher. You'll put boundaries around your degree and become a victim of it.

You may say to yourself, *This is how it has to be done. This is what I know. This is how far I can go.* But you forget that you have so much in you that can't be limited to your job. I often encourage people who attend college not to merely study and look for a job but rather to study and give a job to somebody else.

Successful teachers, plumbers, dancers, landscapers, attorneys, doctors, scientists, farmers, and electricians all have one thing in common: a God-given potential to start something small. If they consider their work important, that motivates them to spend time practicing their craft in order to improve. Eventually they might be more than self-employed; they may provide jobs for others.

Can this happen overnight? I wish that were true. It takes tenacity, patience, courage, zeal, boldness, and audacity to stick to your conviction. Unless you strive to nurture your dreams as time goes by, your dreams will die.

How can we reach for that? When you're bold, courageous, and patient about doing something, you can be compared to an athlete who runs with patience. Can one run with patience? Of course. We all know that running is an action, but patience is an attitude. You should strive to fulfill your calling with a positive attitude. Your attitude will keep you on course, even when you have to make changes. People with negative attitudes give up easily. As Christians, we aren't among those who give up easily; we are relentless because we've realized that God put something in us that will surely be delivered to the world.

Do you think God created us to just go to college, earn a degree, get a job, pay a mortgage, and then die only to leave the same cycle to our children? I don't. I know there's something better.

God didn't breathe His life into us to drag through the day. He didn't create you and me in His image, and crown us with His power, just so we could get by, pay bills, and then die. Always remember that there is something better. Settle not for good when the best is possible, and don't just say a task is done when perfection is possible.

What would happen if scientists had said, "Let's just be content with the nineteenth century's research"? It would have been impossible to send astronauts to space, for one thing. And what about medical science? A whole lot of sicknesses and diseases have cures now which used to be nightmares. Why? Because those in research didn't relent. Do you have any idea how long it took to find the cure for tuberculosis, for example? What if the doctors had said, "This cure is nowhere to be found. Let's do something else." If they had, there would be no cure today. For that matter, I strongly believe that we are headed toward finding the cure for AIDS.

In agriculture, if you wanted to spray insecticide over five acres of corn field, you used to need a full day and fifteen to twenty hired workers. Today, one person can do it in less than thirty minutes with the help of technology. Think of the automobile industry. There's no way to compare the automobiles of a hundred years ago with modern vehicles. When you drive today, you can get where you're going and enjoy the drive. Back then, the car would take you wherever you needed to go, but it wasn't much fun; the car looked and felt like a chariot.

We don't despise what already exists, but we take what we find and make it big—make it great! If we can do better—and I know we can—why should we limit ourselves to good when the best is possible?

Monday into Friday

If you had a chance to survey a random group of people, asking them which day of the week (Monday through Friday) they like most, I'm certain some ninety-eight percent would answer Friday. Do you know why? One reason is that lots of the people hate their careers, simply because the job is hard.

Monday is a hated day, as it's the first day of the workweek. Thus, stress is inevitable. Medical researchers have found out that seventy-five percent of those people who die from heart attacks, die on Monday mornings between 6:00 a.m. and 9:00 a.m. There are also far more people who call in sick on Monday than any other day.

It's all set up in our systems. We've programmed our subconscious to feel weak and lazy on Monday. Unlike others, I like every single day, because I understand that a day is a gift from God. I don't take a day lightly. In fact, my favourite day is Monday. I'm joyful and full of energy on Mondays.

We can never live happy lives hating what we know we'll be doing for years, if not the rest of our lives. If you can do something about it, go ahead and change your job. But if not, embrace it. Liking or hating what you do isn't the issue. Your attitude is. A large number of people don't like what they do, but having a good attitude helps those around you—and yourself as well. When we hate what we do, we automatically sabotage our time. We send negative messages to our subconscious, coming up with words like "This is a bad day." Who told you that? I don't agree with it.

Every day is a God-given day. We call them bad days because we're forced to do something we don't like. Most of the time, it's not even what we do; rather, it's our perception. As the expression goes, "Another day, another dollar." But I say, "Another day, another grace."

If you change your perception, you'll be able to like your Mondays as much as your Fridays. That will help you approach your career with a positive attitude. As it is said, your attitude determines your altitude.

A lot of people dislike their careers because they don't know the distinction between a career and a purpose. Your career is what you do for living, but your purpose is what you're living for. Let's say, for example, that you know you're meant to be a teacher; you know it from the bottom of your heart. Unfortunately, the only position available for you is to lay bricks in a construction company. You may lay bricks for a while. If you do it for a long time, you'll be stressed out, as it's not what you were called to do. Your job will always be a burden.

When you find your mission or purpose in life, you come to enjoy every single day. Moreover, when your purpose turns out to be your career, you'll be thrilled to another level. Even those around you will think you've come from a different planet. Discovering your purpose will help you enjoy every single day of the week, including Monday.

You Are Not Omniscient

One of God's attributes is omniscience. God alone is all-knowing, so you can't try to explain everything. Some things will always be out of your understanding, and no matter how hard you try, they will never be fathomed; they will remain mysteries.

For example, on January 12, 2010, an earthquake struck Haiti, destroying everything in its way, taking hundreds of lives and leaving many more injured and homeless. Haiti is known to be among the poorest countries on earth. What do you say about this catastrophe? What do you think? Scientists explain what they believe to be the cause, but are they totally correct? There are those who say that Haiti made a treaty with the devil, which is why such things happen. Give me a break! Sometimes we have to accept that we don't know what's going on. Some things are out of our control. The only one who knows it all is God Himself. So, stop trying to explain things you have no clue about. Sometimes it's wise to be quiet.

How do you explain this? A parent dropped off his child at school early one morning. After leaving his job at the end of the day, he excitedly went to pick up his kid.

Unfortunately, the school presented to him the child's dead body. How do you consider or even grasp such a tragedy? This happened to twenty families on December 14, 2012, in Newtown, Connecticut.

How can you have the courage to explain this? Where do you start? When I saw the news of the Newtown shooting on television, goosebumps appeared all over my body. I've been a school bus driver; I see how parents are impatient when it comes to waiting for their children to be dropped off at home. I may tell the parent that their kid isn't on the bus because he didn't ride with me that day. That alone can be hard for a parent to accept. But what if you have to tell the parent that their kid is neither on the bus, nor anywhere else, because he's dead?

I'm convinced that we all have situations in life that we can't explain. You know what you feel and what you saw, but if you try to explain it, people will consider you a fool.

In 1999, I arrived in Canada and entered into the process of becoming a resident. After I became resident, I fell into depression, which led me to be diagnosed with bipolar disorder. At least, that's what they say; I don't agree with them. When you have a so-called mental sickness, instead of calling the ambulance, people would rather call the police. That's the law.

While working at a fast food restaurant as a burger flipper, I suddenly had a surge of strange feelings. I could tell something was wrong. My coworkers called the police. This was the third time I'd had an episode. The police came, and I was handcuffed. To make the long story short, around midnight they put me in the cell. I thought, *If I'm released tonight, I won't go home. I'll stay at the Rideau Mall until morning.* Rideau Mall is one of the largest shopping centres in Ottawa.

To my big surprise, less than two minutes later, a policewoman came to my cell and asked me, "Do you want to go to Rideau?"

What was happening? How had she been able to read my thoughts? How could I explain this to somebody? They would certainly say I'd suffered a hallucination. But why me? The answer: I don't know.

A friend of mine recently asked me, "What do you think about the royal family, about all the wealth they have?"

"You're asking the wrong person," I said. "You know, Prince William did nothing but happen to be born into Buckingham Palace."

In effect, if you're born into a royal family, the least you can become is a prince or princess. It's as simple as that. That's the sovereignty of the almighty God. We can never question Him. We cannot explain it, so we must leave it to the one who has the power above all. Right where you are, you might have situations that are difficult to explain. It's okay. You're not alone.

There's a long list of things that are hard to explain. We have the ability to see, hear, taste, smell, and touch. These are the five senses. Nevertheless, knowing that we aren't omniscient doesn't mean we have to refrain from studying or learning. We have so much to learn, but there are other things we will neither be able to explain or understand.

So, let us learn and study what we can and leave the mystery to Him who is master of all.

TRASH IN, TRASH OUT

We are made by that which we feed. We can't expect to have a healthy body by feeding ourselves soda and fast food every day. We have to control what goes into our stomachs. Our bodies aren't trashcans that will accept just anything. Are we feeding our bodies, or are we just filling our stomachs? Remember, we are what we eat. The same holds true for our thoughts.

That which we see and hear affects our thoughts, and then our thoughts make us believe things, and eventually what we believe helps to form who we really are. We are, therefore, what we think. If what we see and hear is good, good things will come out of our mouths. But if it's trash, trash will come out. If you watch something and keep watching it, before long you'll start emulating it.

One day I heard an interview of a guy in the U.S. who took a gun into a public place and slew a large number of people. The reporter asked him, "How is it that you've killed so many people in a few seconds and you're not even shocked?"

"I feel nothing, because I kill every day," he said.

"You kill every day?" the reporter asked. "What do you mean by that?"

The truth was that this killer played violent video games every single day. Those games were practice, and before long killing became meaningless. He switched from the game to the real world. What he saw every day impaired his judgment.

I once worked at a meat-packing company in Alberta. In this environment, if I made a joke that didn't relate to sex, nobody would laugh. I came to understand that people only laughed about sex. I would look for ways to hide my face to avoid listening, but with no success. I didn't know how long I could go on listening to all that nonsense.

I only had to live with it for a little while, for I soon learned how to protect myself. I made a decision one day that before I left home in the morning I had to make sure that I put enough "good stuff" into my mind. What do I mean by that? I had to listen to either a good sermon or a good motivational speech. I would do that for about forty-five minutes. By doing that, I couldn't be affected by trash.

When you have a positive attitude, trash still comes to you, just as it comes to everyone, but since you're strong enough on the inside, it bounces off you like a basketball. I've realized that you can make me hear what you're saying, but you can't make me listen. You can make me look at you, but you can't make me see you.

Whatever goes into you is what comes out. I've learned that if you want to harvest corn, you better put corn seed in the ground. But you don't need to go to school to figure this out. You can't put beans in the ground and expect a harvest of potato. In the same way, you cannot sow anger and reap love. You cannot sow division and expect unity. It's a natural law; there's no way to escape it, no way to cheat it. Whether we like it or not, we will reap whatever we have sown.

This works the same for everyone, everywhere, at all times. There's no partiality. Galatians 6:7 says that a man reaps what he sows. Thus if we don't want to be surprised by what comes out, let us select carefully what goes in. Because when your input is right, your output will be right as well.

THE POWER OF THOUGHT

Thoughts are very powerful. They are unlimited, unstoppable, and have no boundaries. Your eyes have limits, however, because they can only see to a certain distance. Your ears have limits also, because they can only hear sounds that are close to you. Your body has limits; there are things it cannot do, no matter how hard you try. For instance, you may say, "I will run today without stopping." You would be lying to yourself. You will run, of course, but you'll stop at a certain point as your body becomes weak. Your physical body has limitations, but your thoughts have none.

Take a moment and think about this. Your thoughts can reach places you can't go and do what you deem impossible. As mentioned earlier, a human being has at least sixty thousands thoughts every day. It's possible to spend a day without speaking a word, but it's impossible to spend a minute without having a thought. The speed of thought is even higher than the speed of light—and the speed of light is 186,300 miles per second!

Being in Canada, I can start imagining that I'm in China or Africa. It won't take me half a second to get there. When you travel to any country and get to the border, the first thing you're asked for is your visa. Not in my thoughts, though. I don't need a visa to imagine that I'm in China. Though I may not be there physically, my thoughts can reach it in the blink of an eye.

Our thoughts have a huge impact on our lives, whether they're positive or negative. Our thoughts can either bind us or free us up.

A young boy came home from school one day. When he got home, before going outside for a football game, he told his mother, "Mom, I think we're going to lose tonight."

"Don't be negative," his mother said. "Rather be positive!"

The young boy shook his head. "I'm positive we're going to lose tonight."

And they did.

Are you free in your thoughts, or are you bound? In America, an experiment was once performed in which an aquarium was divided by a piece of glass. They put a shark in one side and a kind of fish that the shark loved to eat in the other. Once the fish got into the aquarium, the shark was excited—but it didn't know about the glass divider. He quickly approached, but due to the glass he couldn't reach the fish. He tried more than once, and every time he hurt himself by hitting the glass with his mouth. Eventually, he was bleeding. Then the shark got tired and made no move at all. He remained dumbfounded, watching his favourite food just inches away.

The experimenters then removed the glass, so there was no separation between the fish and the shark. To everyone's surprise, the shark didn't move, not even an inch. The conclusion was that the shark still thought there was a barrier, while in reality there was none.

How many times have we said the same thing? How many times have we considered a glass barrier which didn't exist? Most of the time we act exactly like that shark. We try things, and when they don't work to our expectations, we come up with our own conclusion: this will never work. But just because you tried something once or twice with no success doesn't mean it will never work.

Take Thomas Edison, a man we all know and who is hard to ignore. If you don't know about him, turn your lights off and then you'll remember him. Edison invented the incandescent light bulb. Can you imagine the fame he had? You might think he had a lot, but you'd be surprised then to read his biography. The guy failed a hundred times before he found success. Moreover, he was last in school, but today we enjoy the fruit of his inventions every single minute. What would have happened if Edison, after failing ninety-nine times, decided to stop trying? Perhaps we'd still be living with candles in our homes today.

Our minds are the battlefield. If we can lose battles in our minds, we can also win battles in our minds. Sometimes the real-world events in our lives are the result of our own thoughts. We are who we think we are. Proverbs 23:7 says, *"For as [a man] thinks in his heart, so is he."* Let's focus on the right thoughts!

In my thoughts, I have travelled the entire world. In my thoughts, I've seen my purpose in life fulfilled. Does it mean I have this fulfillment in reality? No, but it's way better than thinking I'll never amount to anything.

With the amount of time and energy you spend thinking negatively, you should switch to thinking something positive. Remember that we are who we think we are. In other words, we attract what we think.

There's a supernatural force around us that we'll never be able to see. This power makes sure our thoughts come in alignment with the life we lead. Haven't you experienced this? You think of something and it actually turns out exactly the way you thought it would. So, don't just think anything; think about what you want to see in your life. Philippians 4:8 says,

> *Whatever is true, whatever is worthy of reverence and is honourable and seemly, whatever is just, whatever is pure, whatever is lovely and lovable, whatever is kind and winsome and gracious, if there is any virtue and excellence, if there is anything worthy of praise, think on and weigh and take account of these things [fix your minds on them].*

You should also be aware of the difference between memory and imagination. In effect, your memory replays your past, both good and bad, while your imagination pre-play your future. Let your imagination get you where you want to be, even if you've never been there before.

What Is Fear?

According to the dictionary, one of the meanings of the word fear is "an emotion experienced in anticipation of some specific pain or danger (usually accompanied by a desire to flee or fight)."3 This is the meaning of the word as a noun. But as a verb, fear means something to be afraid of. If you have to be afraid, you have to be afraid of a specific thing. If I come to you and tell you that I fear, your question will be, "What are you afraid of?"

After analyzing all the meanings of the word fear, I've realized that fear is a paralyzer. There's nothing real to it. It's like a rocking chair; it keeps you moving, but you don't go anywhere. Fear usually shows you the worst-case scenarios. Fear will convince you by giving you all the reasons you aren't qualified for a promotion, telling you that you came from the wrong family, that nobody in your generation has ever made such progress. Who do you think you are? Fear will tell you, "Look at the colour

---

3 *The Free Dictionary*, "Fright," January 29, 2014 (http://www.thefreedictionary.com/fright).

of your skin! You have neither a diploma nor a degree!" Fear will tell you that the pain in your body is cancer, the same thing your great-grandmother died from. Fear will tell you that there's no way to live without debt. It will tell you that you'll never be able to get out of debt. It will tell you that everybody is sloppy, so you might as well be like everyone else. Fear will make you believe in a situation that doesn't exist, and probably will never exist at all. Fear will blind you and neutralize you.

In Matthew 14, Jesus walks on the water. Peter looked out across the sea, saw the approaching figure, and asked, "Jesus, is that you?"

"Of course it's me," Jesus replied.

Peter went further by saying, "Lord if it's really you, command me to come to you."

"Come," Jesus said.

Peter then walked on the water, but when he saw the waves and wind, fear came on him and he began to drown.

There's an interesting point to be made here. Peter was a professional fisherman. You cannot be a professional fisherman if you don't know how to swim. The little that I know about fishing tells me that professional fishermen have to go deep into water to place their nets in the right place. This tells us that Peter knew how to swim. So why didn't he swim? Because of fear, Peter forgot that he could swim.

We all fear to do things at one time or another, but we have to do them anyway. Don't let fear lie to you any longer. Studies show that ninety percent of the things we fear never happen. We shouldn't put our faith to fear. Every time we give in to fear, we activate the fear and allow it to come to pass.

Whenever you see the potential for something to go wrong, refrain from dwelling on the details. I want to know about a situation, yes, but I don't want to know every single detail, especially those details aren't good. By knowing all the details, instead of having faith, you feed your fear.

Let's say, for instance, that your doctor announces to you that you might have cancer. You have two choices. You may focus on people who had cancer but overcame it and got healed. Or you could choose to do the exact opposite, by going into the library to conduct careful research, finding every book that tells you how deadly cancer is. Perhaps it's not cancer that will kill you, but your fear of it.

I once heard of a young man who had lots of unresolved issues in his life. He tried his best to resolve them, with no success. One day, he left his family and decided to bring his life to an end; for him, death was the only option. He had to run away from his problems. He went to the highest bridge in the city in order to jump and die. Before he jumped, another man saw him and came close, expecting either to convince the man not to jump or forbid him from ending his life.

"What's the matter?" the rescuer asked. "Explain it to me, and maybe I can help you."

The guy started explaining his problems, right down to the smallest detail. Before he finished, the man who was listening realized that he, too, must jump. They joined hands, and both of them jumped.

The first lesson is this: don't try to listen to negative situations to the smallest detail. It will pull you down instead of lifting you up. The second lesson is this: if you're running from your problems, you'll give into fear.

The guy who decided to jump off the bridge was killed by his fear of the problems, not the problems themselves. That's the side-effect of fear. Fear will take away your power and strength, as you cannot be fearful and strong at the same time. You can't even think right when you're frightened. Your ability to do right decreases when you act upon fear. In other words, fear will bias your entire decision-making process.

Fear will hold you back and give you reasons to procrastinate. You'll put off for tomorrow what you know needs to be done right now. Never forget that another tomorrow will show up. Fear will tell you that you need to have everything in place before you start something. No. The right time to start doing what you need to do is today—right now.

The Bible says it this way: *"Behold, now is truly the time for a gracious welcome and acceptance [of you from God]; behold, now is the day of salvation!"* (2 Corinthians 6:2)

Purpose-Driven

What is purpose, and what does it mean to be driven by purpose? A purpose is the reason something exists. When you are driven by purpose, you'll have a reason for every move you make. When you're driven by purpose, you'll realize that your time is calculated in such way that you won't lose even a second. As you realize that there's no time to lose, you become focused. This will keep you from distractions. You'll have no time to engage in vain discussions. You'll know exactly where you're going. You won't stop without a good reason. Patience will be required of you.

In the same way a mother must be able and willing to bear her baby in the womb for nine months, you must know your purpose. It may require sacrifice, though. As a pregnant woman faces restrictions as to what she can do and eat to keep the baby healthy, so you must face restrictions in order to fulfill your purpose. There are things you can choose not to do. There are foods you have to choose not to eat, places you can't go, and people you can't spend time with.

Some foods are very tasty, but in reality they are poisonous. Some places may be wonderful for your friends, but not a good environment for you. Some people's speech is toxic; it's like a contamination. If you listen to them for just a minute, you feel heavy in spirit. If you want to realize your purpose and fulfill it, you may not be able to be "normal," like everyone else. You must get out of the crowd and be yourself. As long as you're still in the flock, you'll struggle to emerge.

Have you ever seen a flock of eagles? The answer would be no. Eagles fly alone, high up in the air and always focused. When you are driven by purpose, you're like an eagle. You'll know how to leave the flock of chickens on the ground and pursue your goal in life.

CONCLUSION

I compare time to a seed. When you look at a seed, what comes to mind? When I look at any seed, I see a plant. A plant is what the seed will become one day. In other words, a plant is the future of the seed. I can say that I see the future of the seed *in* the seed. The future of a seed is not ahead of the seed but within the seed, because all the seed can become is built into it.

The same thing happens with our time. We used to say things like, "I expect a better future in the days to come," but we forget that the future is time; that future is not ahead of us but right inside each one of us. There's no way to dissociate ourselves from our future. We are linked to it. We must stop thinking that the future is somewhere ahead of us. That's not the right way to look at time.

Your future is within you. The tragedy is that with this philosophy, you might think it's okay to be sloppy in life, because the future will manifest itself anyhow. That's wrong. The future is time, and time is potential. Within a seed there is a tree, and the tree is the potential in that seed. Potential is defined as a possibility, a capacity, what is expected to be. It may happen, or it may not, depending on many factors. For example, who's in charge? And in what kind of environment do you find yourself?

The car you drive has the capacity to reach the maximum speed on the odometer. That speed is the potential. Let's say the odometer's maximum speed is 260 kilometres per hour. That's how fast you can go if you run to the limit. That's the potential in your car. You can reach that speed any time you want. Tell me, have you ever reached it before? Probably not, because the speed limit on the road is much lower. But you still have the potential to exceed the speed limit.

This is how our cultures create limits, telling us how far we can go, what we can do and what we cannot, how we should dress, and where we can live. God created us with unlimited potential, and He tells us we can do all things. Which report are we going to believe?

The potential is how far you can go, but going there will depend on your decisions, determination, and dedication. When you look at the speed limit sign, perhaps you think, *I could go faster than that.* Anger arises on the inside of you as you realize that you could do better. Our environments have moulded us to fit in, reducing us to what we call "normal life." If you break the rules, you're called a rebel and are said to have violated the law. Thus, let us consider the unlimited potential we all possess and the most important resource of all—time. How do we make the most of our time?

Time is the most important element in life, because everything begins and ends with time. There is time in everything. There is time everywhere. Most importantly, there is time in every individual. You can use it or lose it, depending on your decision. Let not time expire with you. Grab it. Seize it and make it valuable.

When you buy a can of beans, it will always carry an expiry date. This date tells you how long you have to eat the product before it goes bad. Inside the can is protein, as well as fibres and many other nutritious substances. The sad thing is that all these great nutrients will go to waste if the product isn't consumed before the expiry date.

The same principle applies to your life. You have unlimited potential and opportunity, but you also have a length of time to release the entire package within you. If not, you'll die full of unrealized potential. What a tragedy! Remember: you are supposed to die empty. The world needs what is inside you. Why would you take it to the grave?

About the Author

Cletous Kasombo is a young writer originally from the Congo. He now lives in Calgary, Alberta, Canada. He believes that God created every single human being with and for a purpose. However, for us to fulfill our mission on earth, we need to realize that we possess unlimited potential but limited time. We therefore have to seize our time and make it valuable.

Cletous's goal and mission, which he believes to be his purpose in life, is to reach the unreached—the neglected children of the world—with a message of hope, and also to help them realize that they can have dreams of their own and fulfill them.

CPSIA information can be obtained at www.ICGtesting.com
Printed in the USA
LVOW06s2048110414

381381LV00005B/20/P